STICK IT!

40 creative ways to have fun with sticky notes

Bridget Dove

photography by Clare Winfield

GIBBS SMITH
TO ENRICH AND INSPIRE HUMANKIND

First Published in the United Kingdom in 2017 by
Kyle Books Limited
192-198 Vauxhall Bridge Road
London
SW1V 1DX UK
Text © 2017 Bridget Dove
Photographs © 2017 Clare Winfield

Published in the United States of America by
Gibbs Smith
P.O. Box 667
Layton, Utah 84041
1.800.835.4993 orders
www.gibbs-smith.com

Text © 2018 Bridget Dove
Photographs © 2018 Clare Winfield

Designed by Kyle Books Limited
Printed and bound in China

Library of Congress Control Number: 2017964526
ISBN: 978-1-4236-4991-5

18 19 20 21   5 4 3 2 1

Contents

Introduction

The thing about sticky notes is that they aren't all that sticky, at least not permanently. Once you've reconciled yourself to this fact, the prospect of forty creative sticky note craft projects becomes wonderfully transient; you can't expect a sticky note to stay stuck forever. The projects in this book are designed to fulfill an impromptu creative impulse, requiring no more than the basic contents of your stationery drawer: a hole punch, a stapler, a bit of string, and, of course, sticky notes. Whatever the scale—whether a vast piece of wall art or a tiny piece of origami—the joy is in the simple task of making.

There is a meditative quality to peeling, sticking, and folding. It is calming and absorbing, sometimes frustrating (there is only so much you can ask of a sticky note), but also satisfying. You can't rely on them to be perfectly square (they are not), or to be exactly the same size, so forget about parallel lines and equal gaps, and embrace the creativity in not being precise. The colors could be seen as restrictive, as there are a lot of shades of yellow and pink that are almost identical. If you can lay your hands on brown or dark green sticky notes, then go ahead and create a realistic Christmas tree; for everyone else, we must forge ahead with a neon glow.

And this is the joy; in spite of their shortcomings, it is really surprising what you can do with a sticky note when the mood takes you. In those moments of boredom, procrastination, brain freeze, or creative block, you will probably have a stack of sticky notes on hand, so the best thing you can do is get sticking.

Wall
Art

Emoji

For every emotion there is an emoji. Express yourself.

YOU WILL NEED
- **Sticky notes**
  - 34 (3-inch) orange
  - 62 (3-inch) bright yellow
  - 36 (3-inch) bright pink
  - 5 (3-inch) red
- **A large wall**

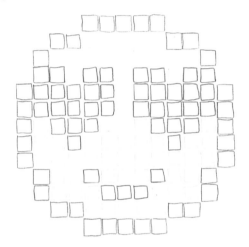

Arrange the sticky notes across the wall as pictured above.

skull

For Halloween/Day of the Dead/just because. There's a bit of fiddly cutting here, but it's worth it.

Cut sticky notes along the dotted lines for each part of the skull as shown here (cont. overleaf).

YOU WILL NEED
- **Sticky notes**
  20 (3-inch) bright blue
  10 (3-inch) orange
  20 (3-inch) bright pink
- **Scissors**

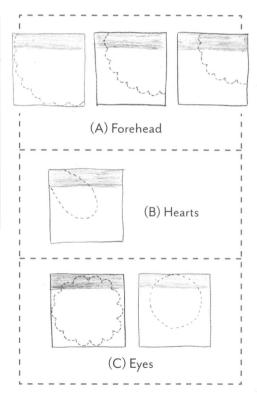

(A) Forehead

(B) Hearts

(C) Eyes

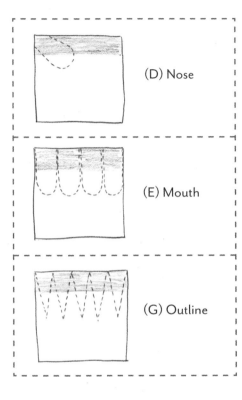

(D) Nose

(E) Mouth

(G) Outline

(A) For the forehead

Arrange a row of whole blue sticky notes and stack the cut blue, orange, and pink sticky notes at each end of the row as shown.

(B) For the hearts

Take six orange, six pink, and two bright blue sticky notes and cut along the dotted lines, then arrange as shown on the chart opposite.

(C) For the eyes

Arrange two whole orange sticky notes, then add two cut bright pink and two bright blue sticky notes as shown to create the eyes.

(D) For the nose

Cut two bright blue sticky notes along the dotted lines, then arrange as shown to create the skull's nose.

(E) For the mouth

Arrange six whole bright pink sticky notes as shown. Cut four bright blue sticky notes and arrange as shown to create the skull's mouth.

(G) For the outline

Cut three bright blue and four bright pink sticky notes along the dotted line, then arrange as shown on the chart overleaf to create the outline of the skull.

CHART

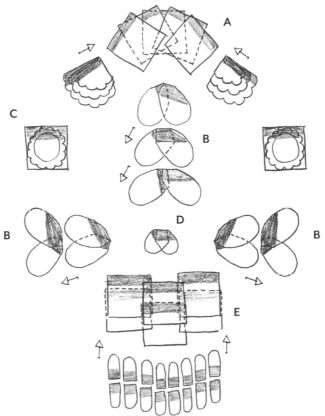

Swallow

YOU WILL NEED
- **Sticky notes**
  About 60 (3-inch) dark blue
  About 60 (3-inch) light blue
  About 60 (3-inch) white
  About 60 (3-inch) turquoise
- **Scissors**
- **A large wall**

This project is deceptively simple and extraordinarily satisfying to create. Continue the scattered sticky notes as far as the wall will allow.

1 Arrange the dark blue sticky notes as shown below, and then trim along the dotted line to create the silhouette of a swallow.

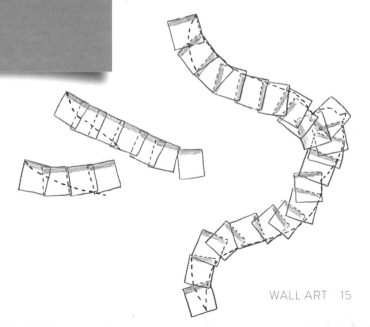

2 Arrange the light blue and white sticky notes as shown below, tucking them in under the dark blue silhouette.

3 Fill in the rest of the swallow with a mix of white, light blue, and turquoise sticky notes, randomly mixing the colors. Spread the sticky notes across the wall to give a scattered effect of the bird in flight.

Dayplanner

This is a genuinely functional project—the beauty is that you can scrap memos and appointments as they change, avoiding annoying crossings out.

YOU WILL NEED
- **Sticky notes**
  62 (3-inch) in an array of colors of your choice
  28–31 (3-inch) yellow
  16 (2-inch) in an array of colors of your choice
- **Scissors**

1 Stick a row of seven different-colored sticky notes on your wall, then stick a row of yellow notes underneath. Repeat until you have enough sticky notes for the month.

2 Cut out numbers as needed, and stick them over the multicolored rows in contrasting colors.

3 To create markers, cut along the dotted lines as shown in the illustrations below. Use the blue frame to mark today's date, the orange arrow for appointments, and the heart for special dates.

4 To make a star to mark important dates, stick together four 3-inch sticky notes, twisting each one as you go.

3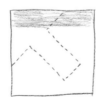

4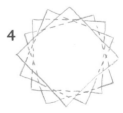

Geometric Tiles

This project is very meditative. It is also really versatile, so choose the colors you love best and keep sticking until you want to stop.

1 Place a sticky note in front of you sticky side down. Using a ruler, draw a line diagonally from the top right corner to the bottom left corner, and another line from top left to bottom right.

2 From where the two lines cross, make a mark 3 cm either side of the center on one of the lines.

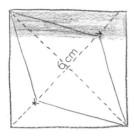

3 Draw a line from each corner to the measured points as shown.

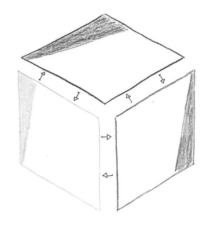

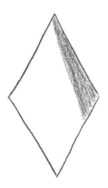

4 Cut out this shape to create a diamond and use this as a template to cut lots of diamond tiles from all the different-colored sticky notes.

5 Stick three different-colored notes on a wall or window in the formation shown above to create a 3D cube. Repeat this pattern as many times as you like, alternating the colors as you go.

Raincloud

This would work just as well on a window or a plain white wall. Swap the raindrops for snowflakes (see page 119) if you are stuck inside when you'd rather be outside building snowmen.

YOU WILL NEED
- **Sticky notes**
  75 (3-inch) turquoise
  100 (3-inch) light blue
  50 (3-inch) white
  100 (3-inch) dark blue
- **Scissors**
- **A large wall**

1 Cut 14 turquoise sticky notes along the dotted line (above) to create raindrops.

2 Stick the light blue and white sticky notes in a 12 × 15 grid as shown in the chart on page 25.

3 Add a layer of white sticky notes, tucking them under the light blue sticky notes to create the top outline of the cloud.

4 Add a layer of dark blue sticky notes as shown, laying them over the light blue sticky notes to create the bottom outline of the cloud. Working upward from the bottom of the cloud, fill in with dark blue and turquoise sticky notes, overlapping them at random until the wall is completely covered. Tuck the final layer under the white sticky notes at the top of the cloud.

5 Stick the raindrops over the white sticky notes as shown on the chart below. Depending on the size of the wall, you can continue to add raindrops to the floor. If you want to cover more wall, simply expand the sky with as many sticky notes as you need.

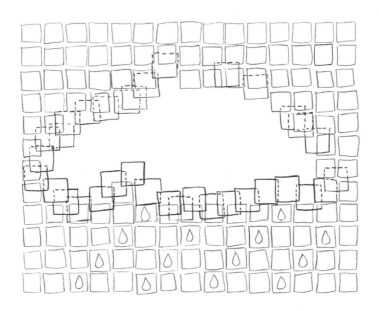

Apple

A really big apple.

Arrange the sticky notes across the wall as pictured.

Cheese Plant

A fast-growing houseplant with wonderful air-cleaning properties, effective in humidifying air-conditioned offices. Here is a variety that doesn't need watering.

YOU WILL NEED

- **Sticky notes**
    25 (3-inch) bright green
    20 (3-inch) light green
    3 (3-inch) mid blue
    6 (3-inch) light blue
- **Scissors**

Use the instructions below and on page 31 to create all the components. Follow the chart on page 30 to arrange all the components on the wall.

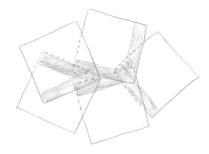

For the leaves

1 To make the leaves, stick together five bright green sticky notes as shown above.

Cont. on page 31.

CHART

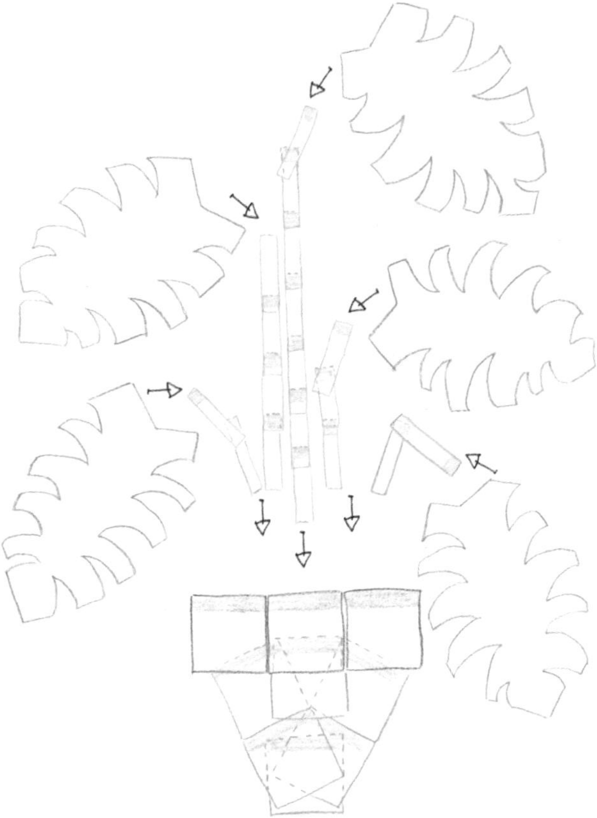

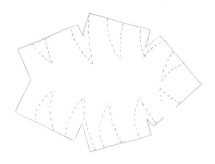

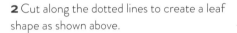

2 Cut along the dotted lines to create a leaf shape as shown above.

3 Repeat steps 1 and 2 to make five leaves.

For the stems
4 Cut 20 light green sticky notes along the dotted lines for the stems.

For the pot
5 Arrange the mid and light blue sticky notes as shown on the chart to create the pot.

Rainbow

YOU WILL NEED

- **Sticky notes**
  Lots of 3-inch bright orange,
  bright yellow, pale yellow, pale
  green, bright green, dark green,
  turquoise, light blue, mid
  blue, dark blue, light purple,
  dark purple, light pink, mid
  pink, and bright pink
- **A very large wall at least
  3¼ × 13 feet**

The chart here gives the core pattern.
Depending on how ambitious you are, this
project can be infinitely expanded—over
walls, floor, furniture, around corners...

Arrange the sticky notes across the wall in a
10 × 45 grid as pictured on the chart on
pages 34–35.

CHART

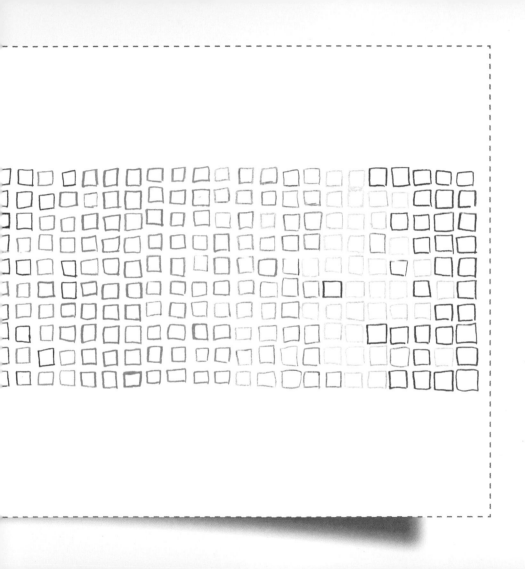

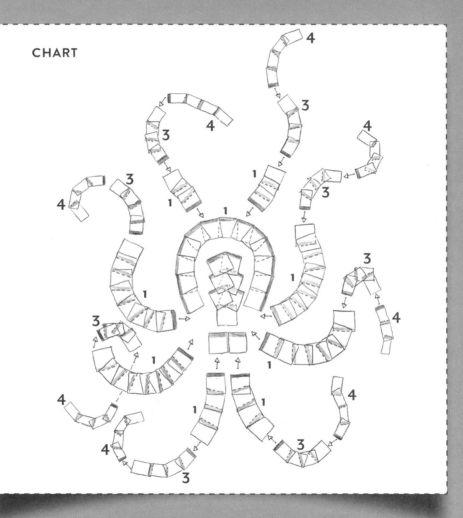

CHART

Octopus

I used the inside of a roll of tape, a stick of glue, and a coin to give the circle sizes for the suckers. They don't need to be particularly precise; a bit wobbly gives a better effect.

YOU WILL NEED
- **Sticky notes**
  100 (3-inch) turquoise
  77 (3-inch) neon pink
  44 (3-inch) red
  2 (3-inch) yellow
- **Scissors**

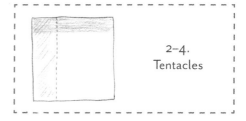

2–4.
Tentacles

For the tentacles

1 Arrange 22 whole turquoise sticky notes as shown opposite to form the octopus's body.

2 Cut 32 turquoise sticky notes along the dotted line shown above. Place the shaded area to one side.

3 Arrange the cut sticky notes to create the thick end of the tentacles as shown opposite.

4 Take the shaded area of the cut turquoise sticky notes and arrange as shown opposite to create the thin end of the tentacles.

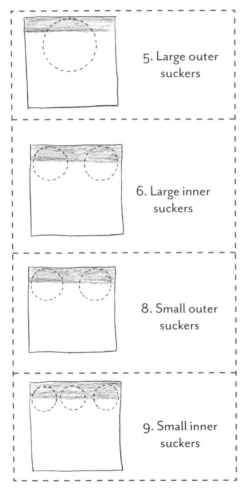

5. Large outer suckers

6. Large inner suckers

8. Small outer suckers

9. Small inner suckers

For the suckers

5 Cut 36 neon pink sticky notes along the dotted line to create 36 large outer suckers.

6 Cut 18 red sticky notes along the dotted lines to create 36 large inner suckers.

7 Stick the red circles on top of the neon pink circles to make the octopus's larger suckers and arrange as shown opposite.

8 Cut 39 neon pink sticky notes along the dotted lines to create 78 small outer suckers.

9 Cut 26 red sticky notes along the dotted lines to create 78 small inner suckers.

10 Stick the red circles on top of the neon pink circles and arrange as shown opposite to finish off the octopus suckers.

CHART

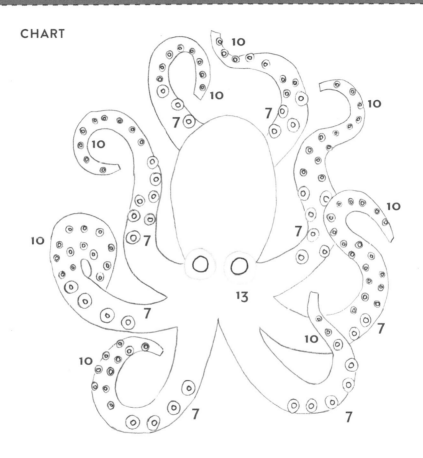

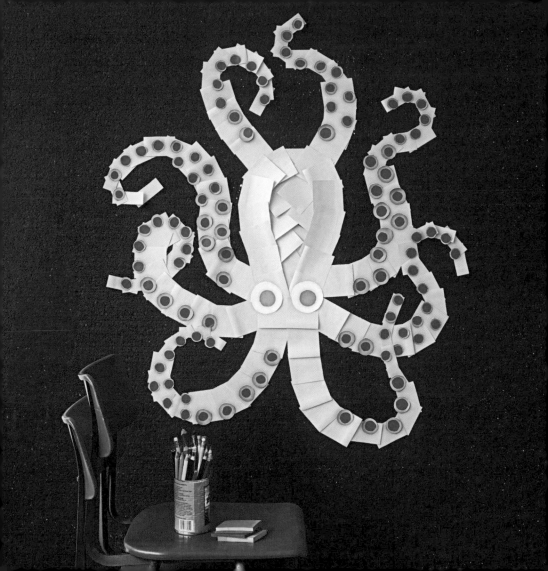

For the eyes

11 Cut two yellow sticky notes along the dotted line to create outer eyes.

12 Cut two neon pink sticky notes along the dotted line to create inner eyes.

13 Stick the neon pink circles on top of the yellow circles and arrange as shown to create the octopus's eyes.

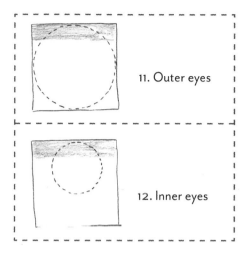

11. Outer eyes

12. Inner eyes

Peacock

Of all the projects in this chapter, this is the most involved but also the most impressive. Prep all your elements first before you start sticking.

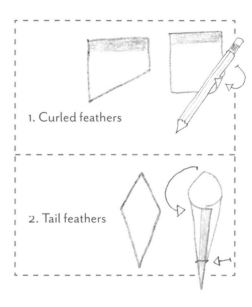

1. Curled feathers

2. Tail feathers

YOU WILL NEED
- **Sticky notes**
  86 (3-inch) dark blue
  18 (3-inch) mid blue
  38 (3-inch) light blue
  30 (3-inch) bright green
  20 (3-inch) yellow
  4 (3-inch) purple
  1 (2-inch) mid blue
  8 (2-inch) yellow
- **Pencil**

Starting with the neck, arrange the sticky notes across the wall as pictured on the chart on page 45, then add the head components.

For the curled feathers
1 Roll a sticky note around a pencil from the bottom corner to create a curl.

For the tail feathers
2 Roll a sticky note into a cone with the sticky strip on the outside, then staple it to secure.

TO MAKE PEACOCK HEAD COMPONENTS

A For the crest feathers

1 Place one dark blue 3-inch sticky note in front of you with the sticky side down, then accordion fold along the dotted lines as shown.

2 Crease across the dotted lines to create an angle.

C For the beak

Place one mid blue 2-inch sticky note in front of you with the sticky side up, then fold it in along the dotted lines.

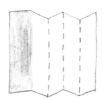

D For the eye

1 Place one yellow 2-inch sticky note in front of you with the sticky side down, then accordion fold along the dotted lines.

2 Crease across the dotted lines to create an angle.

B For the crest base

Place three light blue 3-inch sticky notes in front of you with the sticky side down, then accordion fold each note along the dotted lines as shown.

CHART

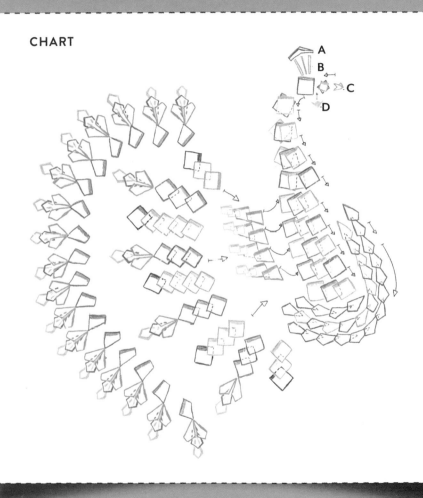

Numbers

If you ever need to create giant numbers, here is how to do it with a little help from the stationery drawer.

Arrange the sticky notes across the wall as pictured on the charts on pages 48–52.

pages 48–52

YOU WILL NEED

- **Sticky notes**
  Depending on the number –
  60 (3-inch) bright pink
  30 (3-inch) mid pink
  60 (3-inch) light pink
  40 (3-inch) light blue
  60 (3-inch) turquoise
- **A very large wall**

CHART

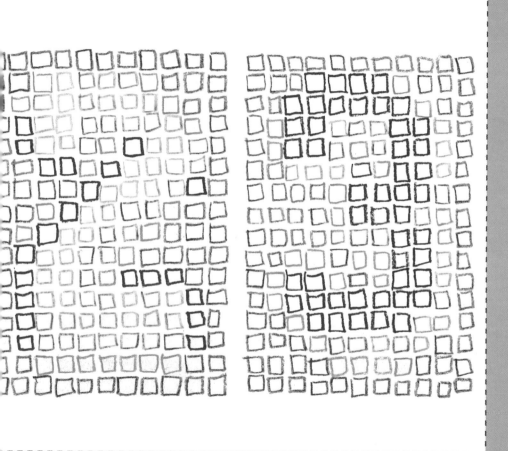

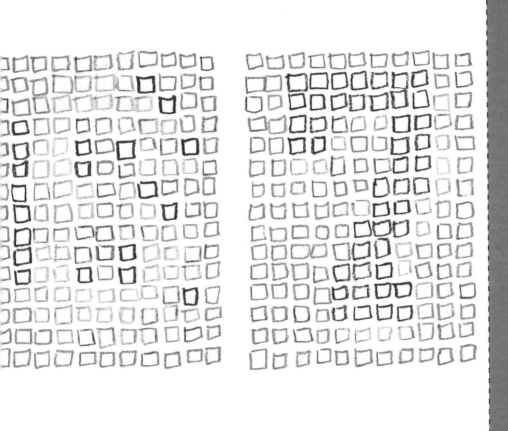

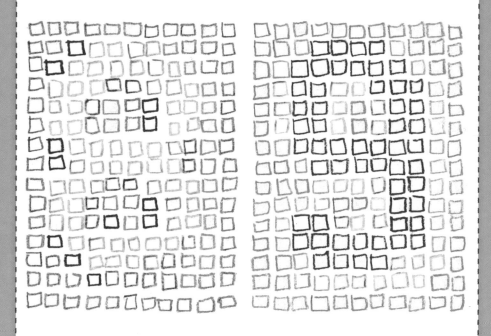

Birthday Cake

Cake is mandatory for a birthday. This one isn't edible, but it looks very pretty.

YOU WILL NEED
- **Sticky notes**
  40 (3-inch) neon pink
  21 (3-inch) light pink
  10 (3-inch) mid blue
  5 (3-inch) neon yellow
- **Scissors**

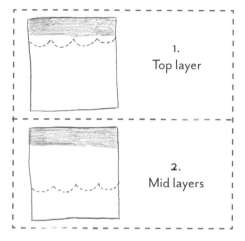

1.
Top layer

2.
Mid layers

For the cake layers

1 For the top layer, cut 12 neon pink sticky notes along the dotted line.

2 For the mid layers, cut 14 light pink and 14 neon pink sticky notes along the dotted line.

3 Stick the top and mid layers, along with whole sticky notes, to your wall as shown on pages 54 and 56 to create the cake.

CHART

1

2

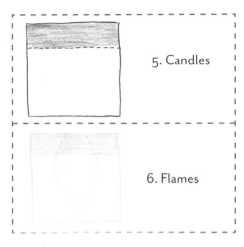

5. Candles

6. Flames

4 To straighten the edges, trim away the excess paper, following the shape of the dotted line on page 56.

For the candles
5 Cut ten mid-blue sticky notes along the dotted line, then stick to the wall as shown on page 56.

For the flames
6 Cut five neon yellow sticky notes along the dotted line, then add to the candles as shown on page 56.

CHART CONT.

6

5

4

Christmas Tree

When a real live Christmas tree is not an option, a stickable one is the next best thing.

YOU WILL NEED
- **Sticky notes**
    - 48 (3-inch) mid green
    - 12 (3-inch) light green
    - 10 (3-inch) bright pink
    - 2 (3-inch) bright blue
    - 5 (3-inch) yellow
    - 2 (3-inch) orange
- **A large wall**

Use this key and the instructions overleaf to create all the components. Follow the chart opposite to arrange all the components on the wall.

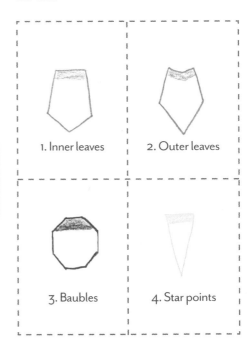

1. Inner leaves

2. Outer leaves

3. Baubles

4. Star points

CHART

For the inner leaves

1 With the sticky side up, fold in half along the dotted line to crease, then unfold. Crease along the angled dotted lines and pinch together to create an angle.

For the baubles

3 With the sticky side up, fold the corners in along the outer dotted lines to create a point. Fold again along the inner dotted lines.

For the outer leaves

2 With the sticky side up, fold the corners in along the dotted lines to create a point. Then fold in half along the dotted line and crease along the top dotted lines to create an angle.

For the star points

4 With the sticky side up, fold the corners in along the outer dotted lines to create a point. Then fold in again along the inner dotted lines.

Origami

4 × 4 Sticky Note Square

This is the base for most of the origami projects.

YOU WILL NEED
- **Sticky notes**
  4 (3-inch) in a color of your choice

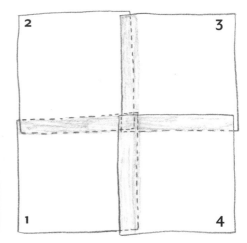

1 Place sticky note 1, sticky side up, in front of you with the sticky side on the right.

2 Add sticky notes 2, 3, and then 4 sticky side down, rotating the sticky side ninety degrees clockwise with each addition, as shown above.

Lotus Flower

A simple, absorbing, classic origami task.

YOU WILL NEED
- **Sticky notes**
  1 Sticky Note Square in a color of your choice (see opposite)

1 Fold along each of the dotted lines and then unfold to create creases.

2 Fold each corner into the center.

3 Fold each corner into the center again, and then turn over.

1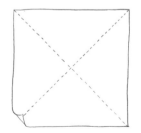

2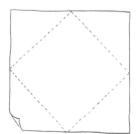

3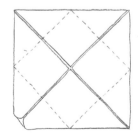

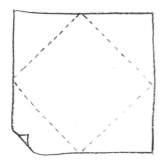

4 Fold each corner into the center along the dotted lines.

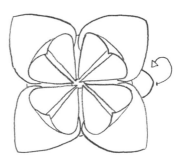

6 Fold the remaining flaps up from underneath to create four more petals.

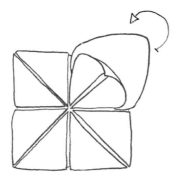

5 Press along the corners to curl them up and fold up the flap from underneath to create a petal.

7 Peel up the four flaps in the center to create the remaining petals.

Hyacinth

These don't have to be neon—you could go for more traditional pinks and purples if you prefer or whatever you have on hand.

YOU WILL NEED
- **Sticky notes**
  Per stem
  4 (3-inch) bright green
  3 (3-inch) bright orange, pink, or yellow
- **Scissors**

1 Place a bright green sticky note, sticky side up, in front of you and then roll it up from the corner.

2 Press firmly to stick and repeat with two more bright green sticky notes.

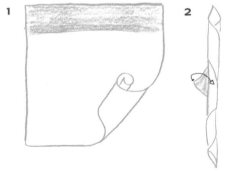

3 Tuck each roll into one another as shown above to create the stem.

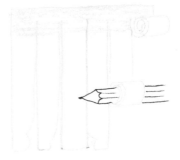

4 Place a bright orange, pink, or yellow sticky note in front of you sticky side down, then cut along the dotted lines to create strips, ensuring not to cut all the way through.

5 Roll each strip around a pencil from the bottom up to create a coil. Repeat steps 4 and 5 with two more bright orange, pink, or yellow sticky notes to create the flowers.

6 Wrap each flower around the stem, working from the top down.

8 Stick two strips together as shown.

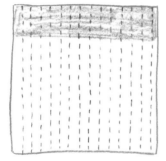

7 Cut a bright green sticky note along the dotted lines to create narrow strips.

9 Loop the strips around the stem to create the leaves. Press firmly to stick to the stem.

10 Repeat steps 8 and 9 above to create two more leaves.

Birthday Card

A recipe for an emergency birthday card, minimum crafting skill, and basic stationery items required.

YOU WILL NEED
- **Sticky notes**
  1 (3-inch) bright blue
  1 (3-inch) yellow
  1 (3-inch) orange
- **Craft knife**
- **Stiff paper or cardboard, cut into two 4 × 6-inch rectangles**
- **Colored tape such as Washi tape**

1 Using a craft knife, cut a balloon shape out of one of the pieces of card.

2 Flip the piece of card over and then stick one blue and one yellow sticky note over the balloon shape.

3 Using a strip of colored tape, secure the two pieces of card together.

4 Write your birthday message on the orange sticky note and then stick it inside the card.

1

2

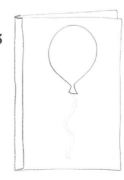

3

Valentines Card

Nothing says I love you like a pink sticky note heart card.

YOU WILL NEED
- **Sticky notes**
  1 (3-inch) mid pink
  2 (3-inch) pale pink
  1 (3-inch) white
  2 (3-inch) bright pink
- **Scissors**

1 Stack together one mid pink, one pale pink, and one white sticky note. Cut along the dotted lines to create three different-size heart shapes.

2 Place one bright pink sticky note, sticky side up, in front of you. Arrange the different hearts along the top, pressing down to stick.

3 Place another bright pink sticky note over the first, sticky side down.

4 Fold both bright pink sticky notes away from each other along the dotted line so that the hearts are on the inside of the card.

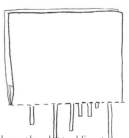

5 Cut along the dotted line to remove the excess heart stems.

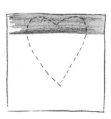

6 Cut a heart shape from a pale pink sticky note, along the dotted line as shown. Stick this on the front of the card.

Frog

I love these—the temptation is to just keep making them so that you have an army of little green frogs.

YOU WILL NEED
- **Sticky notes**
  1 Sticky Note Square in green (see page 64)
  1 (3-inch) white (for the eyes)
- **Hole punch**

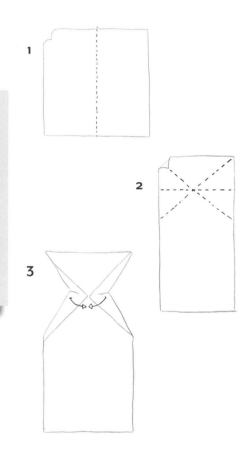

1 Fold along the dotted line.

2 Fold along each of the dotted lines and then unfold to create creases.

3 Bring the horizontal folds together.

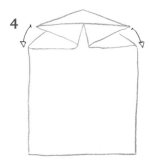

4 Press down flat to form a triangle (the frog's head).

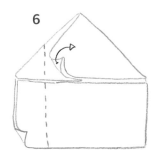

6 Lift the top layer of the left-hand triangle and fold along the dotted line, tucking the side under the triangle. Press flat and repeat on the other side.

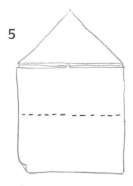

5 Fold upward from the bottom.

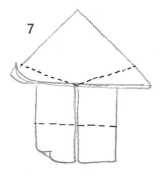

7 Fold upward along the dotted lines into the center.

8 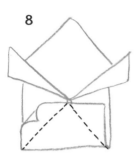 **9** 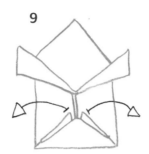 **10**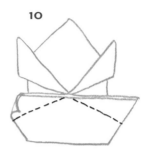

8 Lift the top layer of the bottom left corner and fold down along the dotted lines. Repeat on the right side.

9 Pull the corners out from underneath and press flat.

10 Fold down along the dotted lines and turn over.

11 Fold down along the dotted line.

12 Fold upward along the dotted line.

13 Using a hole punch, cut circles out of the sticky strip of a sticky note and stick to your frog to create its eyes.

11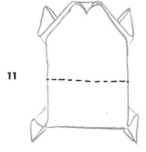

12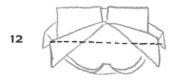

Paper Planes

I struggle to give a practical reason for making these except to say that paper airplanes satisfy a certain tendency in us all to procrastinate.

1 Arrange the sticky notes as shown to create a sheet, using glue to stick down loose ends.

2 Fold inward along dotted lines.

YOU WILL NEED
- **Sticky notes**
  8 (3-inch) in any color
- **Glue**

1

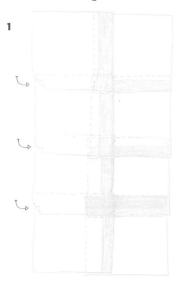

2

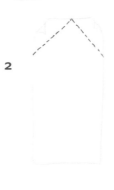

3

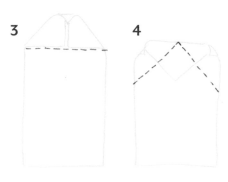

4

5

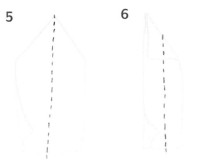

6

7

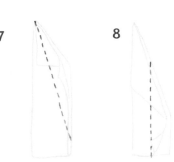

8

3 Fold down along the dotted line.

4 Fold inward along the dotted lines and then turn over.

5 Fold in half along the dotted line.

6 Fold the top layer along the dotted line to crease, then unfold. Turn over and repeat on the other side.

7 Fold the top layer along the dotted line. Turn over and repeat on the other side.

8 Fold the top layer along the dotted line. Turn over and repeat on the other side.

Owl Bookmark

A tricky little number to master, but very satisfying once completed. Have a few spare notes on hand in case first attempts end up in the recycling bin.

YOU WILL NEED
- **Sticky notes**
  1 Sticky Note Square in a color of your choice (see page 64)
  1 (3-inch) in a contrasting color (for the eyes)
- **Hole punch**
- **Black pen**

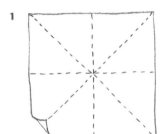

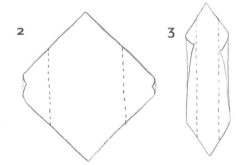

1 Fold along each of the dotted lines and then unfold to create creases.

2 Fold into the center along the dotted lines, then turn over.

3 Fold into the center again.

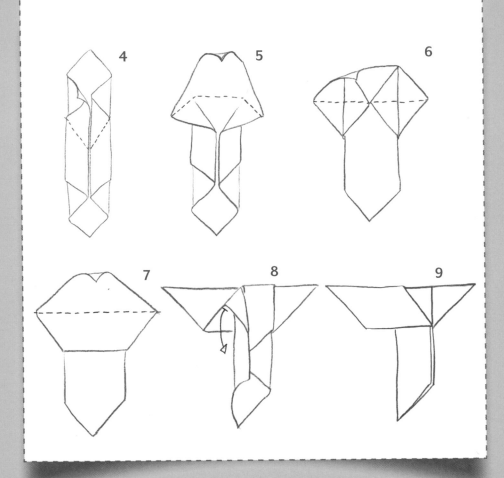

4 Fold outward from the center, along the dotted lines.

5 Fold along the dotted line and press flat. Turn over.

6 Fold down along the dotted line

7 Lift the flap up from behind and fold down along the dotted line. Turn over.

8 Lift the left flap and fold over the right as shown to create a crease.

9 Press flat.

10 Repeat steps 8–9 on the other side.

11 Open out flat and turn over.

12 Open out the left-hand flap from underneath and fold over to the front as shown, inverting the existing creases. Press flat. Repeat on the other side.

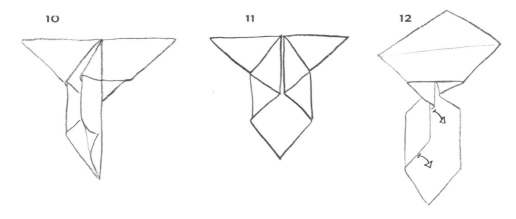

13 Fold along each of the dotted lines and then unfold to create creases.

14 Open out the top triangle and fold the right-hand corner back underneath, inverting the existing creases. Press flat. Repeat on the other side.

15 Fold the top triangle back down to create the ears.

16 Fold along the dotted lines to create the beak.

17 Fold along the dotted lines to crease, then unfold.

18 Open out the right flap and fold inward, inverting the existing creases. Repeat on the left side and then turn over.

19 Fold along the dotted lines to create the tail.

20 Using a hole punch, cut circles out of the sticky strip of a sticky note and stick them to your owl to create its eyes. Use the black pen to add pupils.

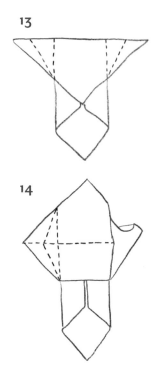

13

14

15

16

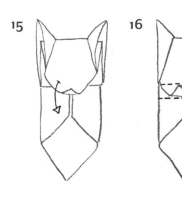

17

18

19

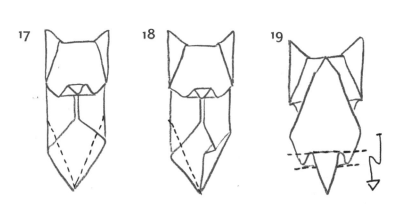

Flickbook

There is something immensely pleasing about a simple flickbook. Make it more elaborate with little flowers or a bit of color. Just add a new element on each page.

YOU WILL NEED
- **Sticky notes**
  A stack of 3-inch sticky notes of your choice
- **Pencil**

1 Beginning with the last note on the stack, draw the plant pot tray.

2 Turn to the next sticky note, trace the pot tray, then draw the top of the pot.

3 Turn to the next sticky note, trace the pot, and draw the stem of the leaf numbered 1.

4 Turn to the next sticky note, trace the pot and stem, then draw the leaf numbered 1.

5 Continue in this way, slowly building up the plant as numbered.

6 Once the drawing is complete, flick through the pages to see the image come to life.

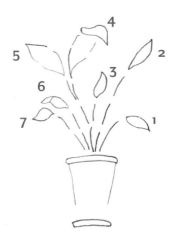

Little Houses

Keep your paper clips and push pins under control. With a bit of dexterity, these houses can be made from individual sticky notes for extra-small boxes.

YOU WILL NEED
- **Sticky notes**
  For the base and roof
  2 Sticky Note Squares in contrasting colors (see page 64)
  For the tiles
  6 (3-inch) sticky notes
- **Scissors**

FOR THE BASE

1 Using one of the sticky note squares, fold along each of the dotted lines in turn and unfold as you go to create creases.

2 Fold inward along the dotted lines.

3 Fold along the dotted lines, folding the bottom third up first and then folding the top third down.

1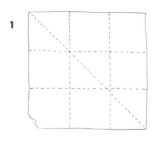

2

3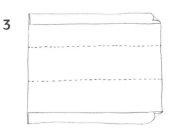

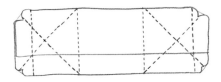

4 Fold along each of the dotted lines and then unfold to create creases. Open out both the top and bottom flaps.

6 Tuck over the top, along the dotted line.

7 Repeat steps 5 and 6 on the other side to create the base of the house.

FOR THE ROOF

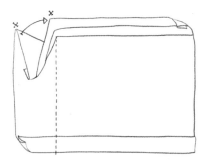

5 Holding the top flap up, fold the top left corner inward, along the existing creases, so that the points marked "X" meet. Repeat with the bottom flap.

8 Using the second sticky note square, fold along each of the dotted lines and then unfold to create creases.

9 Fold along the dotted lines, folding the bottom third up first and then folding the top third down.

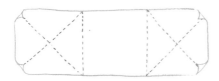

10 Fold along each of the dotted lines and then unfold to create creases.

11 Holding the top flap up, fold the top left corner down so that the two sides meet.

12 Fold the point inward along the dotted line as shown.

13 Repeat steps 4 and 5 on the other side to create the roof. Sit the roof on top of the house base.

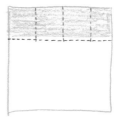

FOR THE TILES

Using the sticky notes, cut along the dotted lines to create the tiles. Stick the tiles to the roof, starting at the bottom and overlapping as you go.

Goldfish

I don't think I have ever seen a spotty goldfish, but as these are made from sticky notes, I think a bit of artistic license can be applied.

YOU WILL NEED
- **Sticky notes**
  1 Sticky Note Square in orange (see page 64)
  1 (3-inch) in a contrasting color
- **Hole punch**

1 Fold along each of the dotted lines and then unfold to create creases.

2 Fold along the dotted line to create a triangle, then turn so that the folded side is at the top.

3 Bring the top right corner to meet the bottom corner and press flat. Turn over and repeat on the other side to make an origami square base.

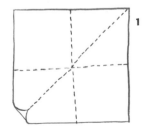

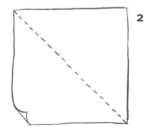

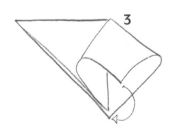

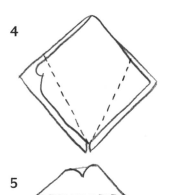

4 Fold the top layer into the center along the dotted lines to create creases, then unfold. Turn over and repeat on the other side.

5 Fold along the dotted line in both directions to create a crease.

6 Open out the top layer from the bottom point and press flat.

7 Fold the top layer up along the dotted lines as shown.

8 Fold inward along the dotted lines.

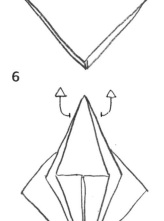

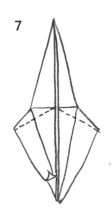

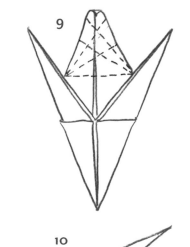

9 Fold along each of the dotted lines and then unfold to create creases.

10 Fold again, along the existing creases, and lift the point up. Press flat to create the top of the tail. Turn over.

11 Fold the right point behind along the dotted line, while folding the left-hand point over. Turn over.

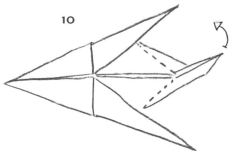

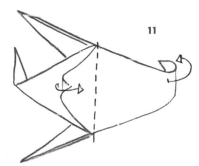

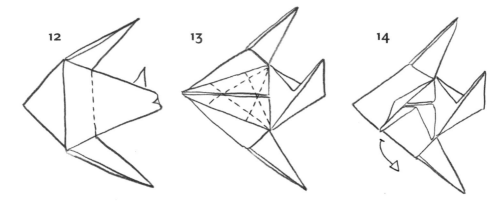

12 Fold the top layer along the dotted line.

13 Fold along each of the dotted lines and then unfold to create creases.

14 Fold again, along the existing creases, pressing the point down. Press flat.

15 Fold the top layer back along the dotted line and press flat to create the bottom of the tail.

16 Use a hole punch to cut circles out of the sticky strip of a sticky note. Use these to decorate the fish.

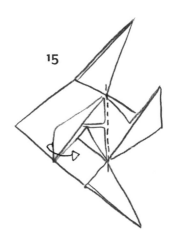

Whiteboard Frame

For inspirational quotes, inspirational poems, shopping lists, to-do lists, to-don't-do lists, and don't-forget-your-lunch-box lists.

YOU WILL NEED
- **Sticky notes**
  - 50 (3-inch) dark blue
  - 24 (3-inch) light blue
  - 18 (3-inch) bright orange
  - 8 (3-inch) bright pink
  - 20 (3-inch) bright yellow
  - 12 (3-inch) light green
- **A whiteboard or blackboard**
- **Scissors**

1 Take one sticky note, place sticky side up, and fold along the dotted line.

2 Fold the sticky corners down to the outside along the dotted line.

3 Cut along the dotted line to create an angle.

4 Turn the sticky note over so that the sticky side is down.

5 Stick to your whiteboard and arrange as shown below.

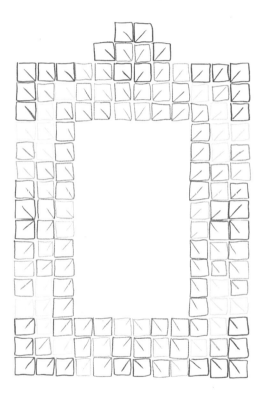

Tree with Falling Leaves

A charming way to creatively store your thoughts.

YOU WILL NEED
- **Sticky notes**
  Lots of 3-inch in colors of your choice
- **A bare branch**

1 Take your branch and place near or over your desk.

2 Write your important memos on the sticky notes and stick to the branch to give the effect of leaves.

Butterfly

A bit like the frogs, you'll want to make more than one. Sticky note colors really lend themselves to this project too.

YOU WILL NEED
- **Sticky notes**
  1 Sticky Note Square in a color of your choice (see page 64)
  1 (3-inch) in a contrasting color
- **Scissors**
- **Hole punch**

1 Accordion fold the bottom half along the dotted lines as shown.

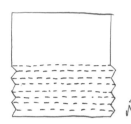

2 Place with the pleats on the left facing down and fold inward along the dotted lines. Turn over.

3 Fold along the dotted lines.

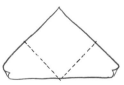

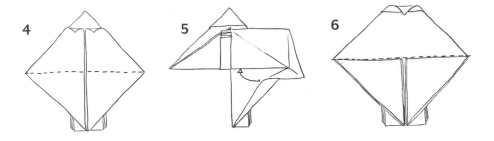

4 Fold the top layer down along the dotted line as shown.

5 Lift the bottom left section while opening out the right-hand triangular flap. Tuck half of the flap underneath itself as shown. Repeat on the other side.

6 Fold down along the dotted line.

7 Fold the top layer back up along the dotted line.

8 Fold inward along the dotted lines, pinching the ends together.

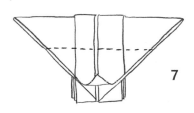

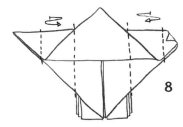

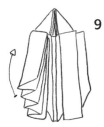

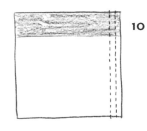

9 Turn over and fan out the pleats to create the wings.

10 Cut two strips from a sticky note as shown above.

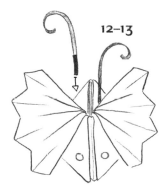

11 Coil each strip around a pencil to create a curl at the end.

12 Stick the strips onto the butterfly as shown to create the antennae.

13 Use a hole punch to cut circles out of the sticky strip of a sticky note. Use these to decorate the butterfly as shown.

Stars

A simple star to hang in a window or wherever you please. Bulldog clips are not compulsory—tape a bit of string to the stars instead.

YOU WILL NEED
- **Sticky notes**
  2 Sticky Note Squares in the same or contrasting colors (see page 64)
- **Scissors**
- **Glue**

1 Fold along each of the dotted lines and then unfold to create creases.

2 Cut along the dotted lines.

3 Fold inward along the dotted lines.

4 For each point, tuck one flap under the other and pinch together. Use glue to fix.

5 Repeat steps 1–4 to create a second star, and then stick the flat sides of the two stars together to create an eight-pointed star.

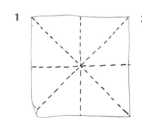

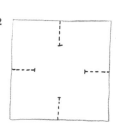

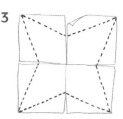

Advent Calendar

Even grown-ups need advent calendars. If you "accidentally" eat all the treats, the envelopes are easily refilled. No one will need to know.

YOU WILL NEED
- **Sticky notes**
  6 (3-inch) bright green
  2 (3-inch) light green
  4 (3-inch) bright pink
  6 (3-inch) red
  6 (3-inch) bright yellow
- **A marker or pen**
- **Small wrapped candy, such as chocolate coins or toffee candy**

1 Take one sticky note, place sticky side down, and fold along the dotted line.

2 Still with the sticky side down, fold the corners into the center along the dotted lines. Fold the left first and then the right, and press to stick together.

3 Repeat until you have 24 little envelopes. Number them 1–24 and stick on the wall. Insert a candy in each one.

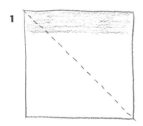

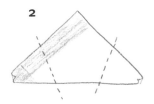

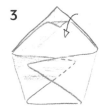

Decorations

Daisy Chains

A more elaborate garland, but delicate and pretty, and well worth the scissor time.

YOU WILL NEED
- **Sticky notes (as many as you like)**
  3-inch yellow
  3-inch white
  3-inch green
- **Scissors**

1 Take one sticky note and place sticky side down. Fold upward along the dotted line.

2 Fold left to right along the dotted line.

3 Fold up along the dotted line.

4

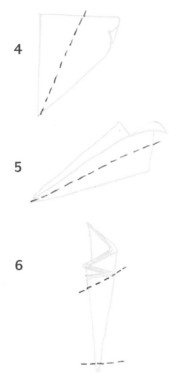

5

6

4 Fold upward along the dotted line.

5 Fold the top layer down along the dotted line, turn over, and repeat on the other side.

6 Cut along the dotted lines.

7 Open out flat, and then cut along the dotted lines to create a daisy.

8 Repeat steps 1–7 until you have the desired number of daisies for your chain.

9 Cut another sticky note along the dotted lines to create strips.

10 Thread each strip through the center of each daisy and string them together to make a chain.

7

9

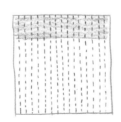

10

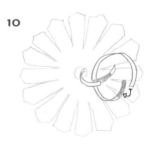

Snowflake String Lights

This is an adaptation of the classic paper snowflake—as little lanterns, they give a blue wintry glow.

YOU WILL NEED
- **Sticky notes (per light)**
  2 (3-inch) turquoise, mid blue, or light blue
- **Scissors**
- **String lights, also known as fairy lights**

1 Take one sticky note and place sticky side down. Fold along the dotted line.

2 Fold along the dotted line.

3 Fold along the dotted line.

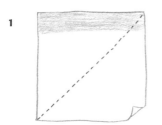

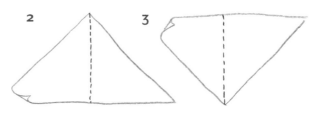

4 Cut along the dotted lines.

5 Unfold to create a snowflake.

6 Repeat steps 1–5 with another sticky note.

7 Place one snowflake behind a bulb on the string of lights with the sticky side up. Lay a second snowflake over the first, sticky side down. Press them together firmly to stick. Repeat until you have covered the bulbs on a string of snowflake lights.

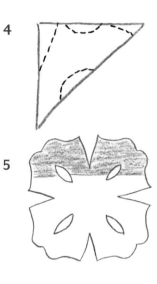

Phone Lanterns

If you don't have a phone with a light, then use a bike light, a tea light, or a flashlight, or make lots for a string of lights.

YOU WILL NEED
- **Sticky notes**
  5 (3-inch) yellow (or any color of your choice)
- **Scissors**

1 Place five sticky notes in front of you, sticky side down, and then cut along the dotted lines.

2 Layer the sticky notes in one long line, leaving about ¾ inch between each, then press firmly to stick them together.

3 Roll into a cylinder and press firmly to stick the ends together. Place over your phone light to create a lantern.

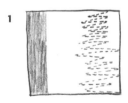

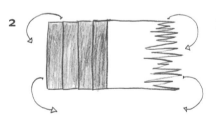

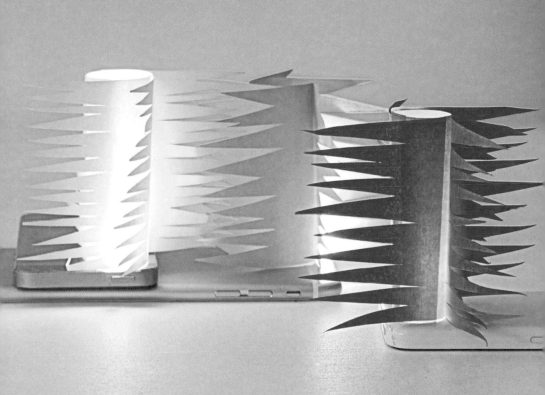

Desk Lamp

If you're going to while away the moments covering things with sticky notes, you might as well put some effort in and create a work of art.

1 Using a ruler, tear all the sticky notes into three pieces along the dotted lines.

2 Starting at the rim of the lamp shade, stick the torn strips in concentric rings around the outside of the shade.

3 Continue to layer the strips in bands of overlapping color—mid blue, light blue, white, pink, white, then light blue at the top.

4 Stick one row of pink around the inside of the rim of the lamp shade to finish off.

YOU WILL NEED
- **Sticky notes**
  20 (3-inch) bright pink
  10 (3-inch) mid blue
  40 (3-inch) light blue
  10 (3-inch) white
- **Ruler**
- **Anglepoise desk lamp or similar**

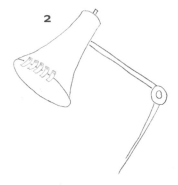

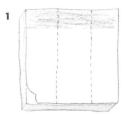

chandelier

This chandelier will hang from an existing light fitting. Alternatively, simply hang it on its own as a decoration. You can make the chandelier as long or as multicolored as your room requires.

YOU WILL NEED
- **Sticky notes**
  120 (2-inch) light pink
  60 (2-inch) dark pink
  40 (2-inch) light blue
  40 (2-inch) bright yellow
- **Scissors**
- **Stiff cardboard**
- **Ruler**
- **Stapler**
- **String**

1 Cut four strips of card into 16 × ¾ inch strips. Measure 2 inches in from each end as shown on the dotted line and fold.

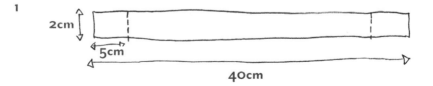

2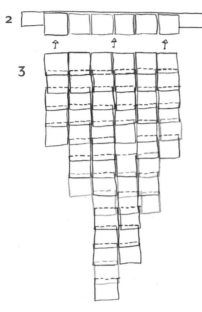

3

2 Stick a row of six sticky notes as shown on one of the cardboard strips.

3 Continue to layer sticky notes in strips as shown to create one side of the chandelier. Repeat on the other three cardboard strips.

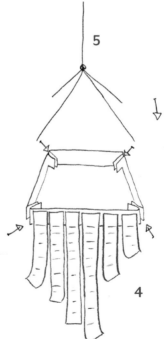

5

4 Arrange the four sides together as shown.

5 Staple the corners together and fix one piece of string to each corner for hanging.

Wrapping Paper

The bow looks complicated but it's a cinch. Who needs ribbon when you've got sticky notes?

YOU WILL NEED
- **Sticky notes**
  For the wrapping paper
  At least 6 (3-inch) in any two colors
  For the bow
  1 Sticky Note Square in a color of your choice (see page 64)
- **Scissors**
- **Glue or tape**

FOR THE WRAPPING PAPER & RIBBON

1 Arrange the sticky notes as shown to create a sheet of wrapping paper. This can be enlarged to the size of your package.

2 Wrap your package using glue or tape to stick. To create the ribbon, cut several strips of sticky notes as shown and stick to your package.

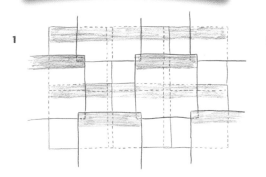

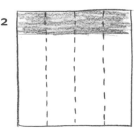

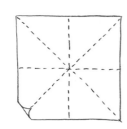

1

2

FOR THE BOW

1 Fold along each of the dotted lines and then unfold to create creases.

2 Fold along the dotted line to create a triangle and turn so that the folded side is at the top.

3 Bring the top right corner to meet the bottom corner and press flat. Turn over and repeat on the other side to make an origami square base.

4 Fold the closed corner end along the dotted line and unfold, leaving a crease.

5 Open out the entire thing and lay flat.

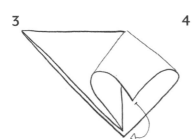

3

4

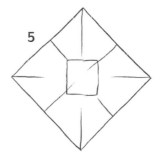

5

6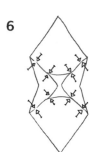

7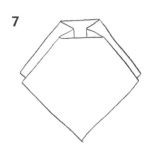

8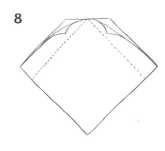

6 Pinch along the existing creases as shown.

7 Press flat as shown.

8 Fold the top layer down along the dotted line as shown. Turn over and repeat on the other side.

9 Open out as shown and cut along the creases marked with a dotted line.

10 Fold the top corner flap along the dotted line.

11 Fold inward along the dotted lines.

9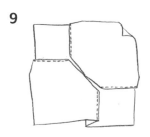

10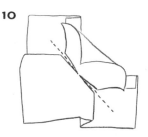

11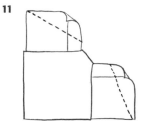

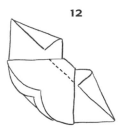

12

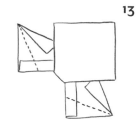

13

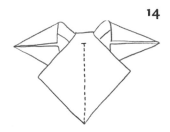

14

12 Fold both layers up along the dotted line as shown.

13 Fold inward along the dotted lines.

14 Cut both layers along the dotted line.

15 Fold both layers inward along the dotted lines as shown, then turn over.

16 Fold inward along the dotted lines as shown, tucking the tip of the bow under the central flap.

17 Cut along the dotted lines to shape the ends of the ribbon.

18 Stick the bow to your package.

15

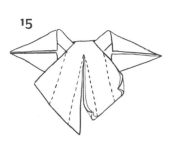

16

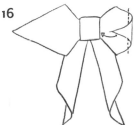

17

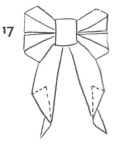

Disco Ball

If you have mislaid your mirror ball, then this is the answer. It doesn't need plugging in and it works in daylight, so win win.

1 Cut the notes into quarters along the dotted lines and discard the shaded area.

2 Wrap a length of string around the ball along the two equator lines, tie together securely leaving a long tail for hanging, and tape to secure.

3 Using the string as a midline, stick the notes around the equator, alternating colors. Continue sticking the notes over the entire ball, spacing them evenly as you go.

4 Hang the disco ball and scatter the wall with more sticky notes to create the effect of disco light.

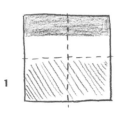

1

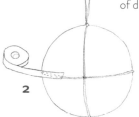

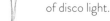

2

3

Table Runner

For when you need an emergency tablecloth. The instructions here are for the core pattern, which can be repeated to fit your table. Start in the center and work outward.

YOU WILL NEED
- **Sticky notes**
  4 (3-inch) dark blue
  12 (3-inch) bright yellow
  8 (3-inch) orange
  12 (3-inch) white
  12 (3-inch) light blue
- **A table**
- **Scissors**

1 Arrange the dark blue, yellow, and orange sticky notes in a 6 × 4 grid, as pictured, in the center of the table.

2 Cut 12 white and 12 light blue sticky notes along the dotted line.

3 Arrange the cut sticky notes on top of the grid as pictured. Repeat the pattern to fill the table and complete your runner, finishing the ends with a row of white and orange.

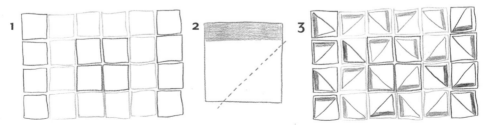

Party Streamers

Last-minute Friday afternoon party streamers.

YOU WILL NEED
- **Sticky notes**
  1 stack of 3-inch pop-up
  (Z-type) sticky notes (designed
  for a dispenser) of your chosen
  color
- **Tape or adhesive putty**

1 Take the top loose end of a pack of pop-up (Z-type) sticky notes and lift to expand and create a streamer.

2 Secure to the wall, ceiling, or filing cabinet using tape or adhesive putty.

Hanging Decorations

Only slightly more involved than the streamers, but still very very easy.

YOU WILL NEED
- **Sticky notes**
  1 stack of 3-inch pop-up
  (Z-type) sticky notes (designed
  or a dispenser) of your chosen
  color
- **String**
- **Stapler**

1 Peel an even number, between six and fourteen, of sticky notes away from the back of the stack, keeping them together.

2 Bring the top and bottom loose ends together to form a flower shape. Press together to stick.

3 Secure a piece of string to the decorations with a stapler for hanging.

christmas Holly

A festive decoration to perk up a dull corner, or make a heap of them and create a wreath, a swag, or a whole holly tree.

YOU WILL NEED
- **Sticky notes**
  2 (3-inch) bright green
  1 (3-inch) light green
  1 (3-inch) bright pink
- **Scissors**
- **Hole punch**

1 Take a stack of two bright green sticky notes, and with the sticky side down, fold along the dotted line.

2 Cut along the dotted line and unfold to create two leaf shapes.

3 Stick these in sprig-like clusters onto a light green sticky note.

4 Using a hole punch, cut a few circles in the sticky area of a pink sticky note. Use these to create clusters of holly berries at the top of the leaves.

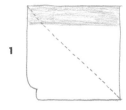 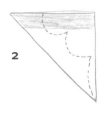 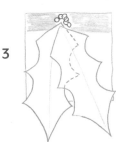

Acknowledgments

Thank you to:
Andy, for being the ideas man and strict quality control, for making sure everything is a good as it possibly can be. Lucy, for your expert folding skills and nonchalant attitude to "the stick." Clare, for your enthusiasm, your brass (if you don't ask you don't get), and, of course, for your skills in taking excellent pictures. Tom, for your very accurate eye and capacity for repetitive sticking. To Claire and Judith and all at Kyle. Also thanks to some anonymous, dusty surveyors for not tidying up in twenty years.